DISABL
BENEFITS 101:

C000155607

How to Apply for and Maximize
DLA and PIP

Teeghan Rhodes

<u>TABLE OF CONTENTS</u>

<u>DISCLAIMER</u>

The information provided in this book, "Disability Benefits 101," is intended for general informational purposes only and should not be considered legal, financial, or medical advice. The author and publisher of this book are not responsible for any actions taken by readers based on the information provided in this book.

It is important to note that laws and regulations related to disability benefits can vary by state and country. The information presented in this book may not be applicable or accurate for all readers, and it is recommended that readers consult with a qualified professional before making any decisions related to their disability benefits.

While the author and publisher have made every effort to ensure the accuracy and completeness of the information presented in this book, they cannot guarantee that the information is free from errors or omissions. Readers should conduct their own research and verify any information provided in this book before relying on it.

Additionally, the author and publisher of this book do not endorse any particular disability benefits program, service, or provider. Readers should carefully evaluate all options and make decisions based on their own unique circumstances and needs.

Finally, readers should be aware that the information presented in this book may become outdated or inaccurate over time as laws and regulations related to disability benefits change. The author and publisher of this book cannot guarantee that the information presented in this book will remain accurate or relevant in the future.

In conclusion, this book is intended to provide a general overview of disability benefits and related topics. Readers should not rely solely on the information provided in this book and should seek the advice of a qualified professional before making any decisions related to their disability benefits.

TEEGHAN RHODES

ACKNOWLEDGMENT

Writing a book is a journey that requires the support, encouragement, and guidance of many people. I would like to take this opportunity to express my gratitude to those who have helped me along the way in creating "Disability Benefits 101."

First and foremost, I would like to thank my family for their unwavering support and encouragement throughout this project. Your love, understanding, and patience have been the cornerstone of my life and this book. I am grateful for your constant encouragement, which has allowed me to pursue my passions and achieve my goals.

I would like to thank my friends who have supported me through the ups and downs of this project. Your unwavering encouragement and positivity have been a constant source of motivation for me.

I also want to extend my gratitude to my editor and the publishing team who helped me shape this book into a coherent and informative resource for readers. Your invaluable insights and feedback have been instrumental in creating a book that I am proud to share with others.

I would like to thank the many individuals who shared their personal experiences and expertise on disability benefits with me during the research phase of this project. Your insights and knowledge have been invaluable in helping me create a comprehensive guide to navigating the complex world of disability benefits.

Finally, I want to express my gratitude to the readers who have taken the time to read this book. I hope that the information presented in "Disability Benefits 101" will help you navigate the complex world of disability benefits and make informed decisions that will improve your quality of life. Your feedback and support are deeply appreciated.

In conclusion, writing this book has been a challenging but rewarding experience, and I am grateful to everyone who has played a part in making it a reality. Thank you all for your support and encouragement along the way.

DEDICATION

This book is dedicated to all those who are navigating the complex world of disability benefits.

To those who have faced barriers and challenges in accessing the resources and support they need to live a fulfilling life, this book is for you.

To the caregivers, friends, and family members who provide support and assistance to those with disabilities, this book is for you.

To the advocates and organizations who work tirelessly to improve the lives of those with disabilities, this book is for you.

Your perseverance, strength, and resilience in the face of adversity are an inspiration to us all. It is my hope that the information and resources provided in this book will help you navigate the complex world of disability benefits and access the support and resources you need to thrive.

Thank you for your unwavering commitment to creating a more inclusive and equitable world for all.

<u>PREFACE</u>

I'm happy to welcome you to "Disability Benefits 101: How to Apply and Maximize DLA and PIP." With particular reference to Disability Living Allowance (DLA) and Personal Independence Payment (PIP), this book is meant to arm readers with thorough knowledge on navigating the murky world of disability benefits in the UK.

As someone who has dealt with the difficulties of applying for and obtaining disability payments, I am aware of the uncertainty, frustration, and fear that can accompany the procedure. However, I am also aware of how crucial these benefits are in terms of giving persons with disabilities the assistance and tools they need to have happy lives.

This book's goal is to serve as a comprehensive manual that will teach readers how to apply for DLA and PIP, comprehend the requirements for qualifying, and maximize their payments. People will be provided with the research, real-life examples, and professional guidance they need in this book to make wise benefit decisions and obtain the support and tools they require to succeed.

An overview of disability benefits in the UK is given in Chapter 1, together with information on the types of benefits that are offered, the requirements for qualifying, and the application process. Chapter 2 looks into the specifics of DLA, including the requirements for qualifying, the application procedure, and the various benefit rates that are offered. PIP is the subject of Chapter 3, which also covers its eligibility requirements, application procedures, and many components.

The significance of medical evidence and how to collect it to support an application for disability payments are discussed in chapter four for readers. Chapter 5 offers helpful advice on how to maximize your DLA and PIP benefits, as well as how to appeal a judgement and handle a change in circumstances.

Chapter 6 of this book provides readers with an extensive compilation of additional resources and organizations in the UK that offer assistance to individuals with disabilities and advocate on their behalf.

It is crucial to bear in mind that the information contained in this book was accurate at the time of its writing. However, regulations and legislation regarding disability benefits may undergo changes as time progresses. Therefore, readers are strongly advised to conduct their own research and seek guidance from knowledgeable professionals before making any decisions concerning their disability benefits.

Last but not least, "Disability Benefits 101: How to Apply and Maximize DLA and PIP" aims to give readers thorough guidance on negotiating the challenging world of disability benefits in the UK. I'm hoping that this book will make it easier for readers to get the resources and support they need to succeed despite their disabilities.

INTRODUCTION

Do you or a cherished individual reside with a disability in the United Kingdom? If affirmative, you are aware that traversing the intricate realm of disability benefits can be an intimidating and overwhelming ordeal. From ascertaining eligibility to completing protracted application forms and grappling with bureaucratic obstacles, the procedure can be exasperating and time-consuming.

Nevertheless, disability benefits are crucial for providing the necessary support and resources to lead a gratifying existence. Henceforth, I have composed "Disability Benefits 101: A Guide to Application and Optimization of DLA and PIP." This literary work encompasses a comprehensive compendium that will equip you with the enlightenment essential to navigate the application process and acquire the benefits rightfully owed to you.

Whether you seek to secure the Disability Living Allowance (DLA) or the Personal Independence Payment (PIP), this publication will facilitate comprehension of the qualifying criteria, steer you through the application process, and maximize your entitlements. By means of personal encounters, expert discernment, and pragmatic suggestions, you will acquire the aptitude to make judicious choices regarding your benefits and access the reinforcement and resources indispensable for flourishing.

Within the pages of "Disability Benefits 101," an elaborate overview of disability benefits in the United Kingdom awaits, encompassing the diverse categories of available benefits and the application course of action. Additionally, you will acquaint yourself with the eligibility requisites for DLA and PIP, uncover practical recommendations for optimizing your entitlements, encompassing guidance on contesting decisions and adapting to changing circumstances.

Furthermore, this literary creation comprises invaluable insights on the significance of medical evidence and strategies for procuring it to fortify your application for disability benefits. Furthermore, you shall encounter an inventory of supplementary resources and organizations that cater to support and advocacy for individuals with disabilities in the United Kingdom.

As an individual who has personally encountered the tribulations of applying for disability benefits, I comprehend the importance of possessing accurate information and receiving adequate support.

Consequently, I have endeavored to pen "Disability Benefits 101: A Guide to Application and Optimization of DLA and PIP." My aspiration is for this literary piece to empower you in accessing the requisite support and resources to lead a gratifying life and prosper in the face of disability-related challenges.

What DLA is and its importance to disabled people?

To help people with disabilities or chronic health conditions pay for independent living, the UK government offers a benefit called Disability Living Allowance (DLA). The program's objective is to provide financial support to the most disadvantaged people in society in order to enable them keep their independence and dignity.

DLA is available to people under the age of 16 who have care or mobility needs, and to people over the age of 16 but under state pension age who have care needs. The benefit is tax-free, and recipients do not need to pay it back.

You can't say enough about how important DLA is for disabled people. Having a disability can be hard in many ways, including when it comes to money. People with disabilities often have to pay for extra things because of their condition, like mobility aids, changes to their homes, and special tools. DLA can help people with disabilities pay for these costs and make sure they can live as freely as possible.

DLA is divided into two components: the care component and the mobility component. The care component is intended to help with the costs of personal care, such as help with washing, dressing, and eating. The mobility component is intended to help with the costs of getting around, such as the cost of a wheelchair or adapted vehicle.

The care component of DLA is divided into three rates: the lowest rate, the middle rate, and the highest rate. The mobility component of DLA is also divided into three rates: the lowest rate, the middle rate, and the highest rate.

The amount of DLA a person can get is based on how much help they need and how much they apply for. For example, the highest rate for the care component is currently £89.60 per week, while the highest rate for the mobility component is £62.55 per week. The money a person gets can be used for a variety of things, like transportation, personal care, and tools.

One of the most notable advantages of DLA is its independence from an individual's financial circumstances. This means that eligibility for the benefit is not influenced by a person's income or savings. This is especially critical considering that many disabled individuals are unable to work due to health conditions and may lack the financial means to support themselves.

DLA also serves as a gateway for disabled individuals to access additional forms of support. By receiving DLA, individuals may become eligible for various other benefits, such as Carer's Allowance, Housing Benefit, and Council Tax Reduction. This expands the range of assistance available to them and enhances their overall support network.

Beyond the monetary assistance it offers, DLA holds the potential to profoundly influence the lives of disabled individuals in various aspects. For instance, receiving DLA can instill a sense of worth and bolster their perception of societal support. Moreover, it plays a pivotal role in enhancing their mental well-being by alleviating financial burdens, enabling access to essential resources, and fostering their ability to lead independent lives.

DLA plays a vital role as a fundamental support system for individuals with disabilities in the United Kingdom. Through its provision of financial aid, it effectively alleviates the extra expenses associated with their conditions, empowering them to lead lives characterized by increased independence and unwavering dignity. The absence of DLA would present numerous obstacles for countless disabled individuals, hindering their access to the essential resources and support required for a fulfilling and contented existence.

Why the Process of Claiming DLA is Overwhelming and Confusing

The process of claiming Disability Living Allowance (DLA) can be overwhelming and confusing for many disabled people. This is because the process is often lengthy and requires a lot of paperwork and documentation, which can be difficult for individuals with disabilities to navigate. In this section, we will explore why the process of claiming DLA can be so challenging and how it can be improved.

The process of applying for DLA can be daunting primarily due to the extensive documentation it demands. Claimants are required to provide substantial evidence of their disability, which includes medical reports, letters from healthcare professionals, and detailed information regarding their daily living and mobility requirements. Obtaining such documentation can be particularly challenging, especially for individuals with multiple health conditions or those who face difficulties in effectively communicating their needs.

The complexity of the eligibility criteria is another factor that contributes to the confusion surrounding the DLA claim process. The assessment involves a series of inquiries concerning an individual's care and mobility requirements. To qualify for the benefit, specific criteria must be met, such as requiring assistance with personal hygiene, dressing, eating, or experiencing challenges with walking and mobility. These criteria can be intricate to comprehend and navigate, especially for individuals with complex or fluctuating needs.

The language employed in the DLA application process can pose confusion for numerous individuals with disabilities. The application forms and accompanying guidance notes frequently utilize technical terminology, making it challenging for individuals to comprehend. This issue can be particularly daunting for those who experience communication difficulties or have learning disabilities.

The evaluation procedure for DLA can generate confusion and anxiety among numerous individuals with disabilities. It entails a face-to-face assessment conducted by a healthcare professional, who poses a series of inquiries regarding the individual's care and mobility requirements. This assessment can be distressing for many disabled individuals, especially if they have had unfavorable encounters with healthcare professionals in the past.

The time it takes to complete a DLA claim can add to the stress and anxiety that comes with being disabled. The benefit's administrator, the Department for Work and Pensions (DWP), has recently come under fire for the length of time it takes to process claims. Some disabled persons have had to wait months, if not years, for a ruling on their claim, which has harmed their finances and prevented them from receiving the assistance they require.

Lastly, the DLA application process can be intimidating for many disabled individuals due to the requirement of disclosing sensitive information about their health and care needs. Discussing such matters can be delicate and challenging, especially for those who have experienced stigma or discrimination in the past. Some individuals with disabilities may hesitate to openly address their condition, which can pose additional obstacles in obtaining the necessary assistance they need.

In summary, the process of applying for Disability Living Allowance (DLA) can be overwhelming and confusing for many individuals with disabilities. The intricate eligibility criteria, extensive documentation requirements, technical language in the application materials, and face-to-face assessments can all contribute to stress and anxiety. To enhance the DLA claim process, it is essential to simplify the eligibility criteria, provide clearer and more accessible guidance, and minimize decision waiting times. Moreover, it is crucial to ensure that the process is sensitive to the needs of disabled individuals, treating them with utmost respect and dignity throughout assessments and decision-making procedures.

The Aim of the Book and What it Hopes to Achieve

The aim of the book "Disability Benefits 101: How to Apply and Maximize DLA and PIP" is to provide a comprehensive guide for disabled people who are navigating the complex process of claiming disability benefits in the UK. The book aims to demystify the application process for Disability Living Allowance (DLA) and Personal Independence Payment (PIP) and to provide practical advice and tips on how to maximize entitlements.

One of the main goals of the book is to address the barriers that disabled people face when claiming disability benefits. As we discussed earlier, the process of claiming DLA and PIP can be overwhelming and confusing for many individuals with disabilities. This can lead to frustration, stress, and anxiety, which can further exacerbate their health conditions. The book aims to provide clear, accessible information about the benefits system and to empower disabled people to navigate the process with confidence.

Lastly, the process of claiming DLA can be a source of stress for numerous individuals with disabilities as it necessitates disclosing personal information about their health and care requirements. This can be a delicate and challenging subject, particularly for those who have experienced discrimination or societal stigma. Some disabled individuals may hesitate to share details about their impairments, which can hinder their ability to obtain the necessary support they need.

The book also aims to provide practical advice and tips on how to maximize entitlements to disability benefits. This includes guidance on how to fill out application forms, what evidence to provide, and how to appeal decisions if necessary. The book will also provide information on how to access additional support and resources, such as local advocacy services and disability charities.

In essence, the book strives to enhance the process of claiming disability benefits for individuals with disabilities in the UK. It seeks to accomplish this by offering transparent, easily understandable information and practical guidance, empowering disabled people to navigate the system with self-assurance and obtain the necessary support to lead fulfilling lives. Additionally, the book aims to foster awareness regarding the significance of disability benefits and advocate for social inclusion and equality for disabled individuals.

In summary, the book "Disability Benefits 101: How to Apply and Maximize DLA and PIP" aims to provide a comprehensive guide to claiming disability benefits in the UK. By addressing the barriers that disabled people face when claiming benefits, promoting the importance of disability benefits, and providing practical advice and tips, the book aims to improve the experience of claiming disability benefits and promote social inclusion and equality for disabled people.

1: UNDERSTANDING DLA

A benefit available in the UK called Disability Living Allowance (DLA) is made expressly to assist people with disabilities in managing the higher costs associated with their condition. Notably, DLA is not means-tested, which implies that neither income nor savings affect the benefit amount. This chapter aims to give a thorough overview of DLA, covering its features, eligibility standards, many components and their coverage, as well as how PIP affects DLA.

Overview of DLA

DLA is a tax-free benefit that is granted to individuals facing disabilities or long-term health conditions. Its purpose is to alleviate the additional expenses associated with living with a disability, including the costs of mobility aids, care services, and other forms of support. DLA aims to provide financial assistance to disabled individuals who require extra aid with their daily living or mobility requirements.

DLA is accessible to individuals below the age of 65, whose physical or mental impairments pose challenges in carrying out everyday activities. The benefit is categorized into two components: the care component, which is provided to individuals in need of assistance with personal care, and the mobility component, which is allocated to those requiring aid in transportation and getting around.

Eligibility Criteria for DLA

Disability Living Allowance (DLA) may be available to people with disabilities who have trouble doing everyday things like getting dressed, taking a bath, or moving around. At least a year has passed since these problems began. For the application to be accepted, the person must have lived in the UK for at least two of the last three years and not be older than 65.

To get the Disability Living Allowance (DLA), a person must meet the requirements for either the movement or care component. To be qualified for the care component, a person must show that they need help with everyday tasks like getting dressed, bathing, and eating. To get the moving component, you have to show that you have a disability that makes it hard to move around. This group includes problems that happen when people walk on streets or use public transportation.

Different Components of DLA and What They Cover

DLA has two parts: the care component and mobility component.

- The care component gives money to people who need help with things like cleaning, getting dressed, or eating. The amount paid for the care component is based on how much help is needed. There are three levels: high, middle, and low. People who need help for a big chunk of the day or night pay less. People who need care or help all day or all night can get the middle rate. People who need help or tracking both during the day and at night have to pay more.

- People who need help getting around can get money from the mobility component. How much is paid for the mobility component depends on how much help the person needs. One rate is lower than the other, and the other is greater. People who have trouble getting around or taking public transport are given the lower rate. People who can't move around much or who can't walk at all get the higher rate.

Changes to DLA due to the introduction of Personal Independence Payment (PIP)

DLA is being phased out for individuals of working age (16-64) in the UK and being replaced by Personal Independence Payment (PIP). PIP has been gradually implemented since April 2013 and aims to provide a more equitable and unbiased evaluation of an individual's specific requirements.

PIP evaluates individuals' capacity to perform a variety of everyday activities and their ability to manage their daily living and mobility requirements. This assessment employs a points system, where the amount of benefit received is determined by the number of points awarded to the individual. The points are assigned based on the level of assistance required to carry out the activities outlined in the assessment.

The PIP assessment is conducted by a healthcare professional who will inquire about the individual's capabilities in various activities. The assessment encompasses several areas, such as mobility, daily living, and cognitive or mental health conditions.

Mobility activities encompass tasks such as navigating indoor and outdoor environments, utilizing stairs and public transportation, and organizing and executing journeys. Daily living activities encompass responsibilities like food preparation, personal hygiene, dressing, and medication management. Additionally, cognitive abilities and mental health conditions, including memory and decision-making, are also considered during the assessment.

The PIP assessment can be a source of stress for numerous individuals, especially those with mental health conditions or concealed disabilities. Articulating the impact of their condition on everyday life can be challenging, and some individuals may experience anxiety or feelings of being overwhelmed throughout the process.

It is crucial to remember that PIP is not means-tested, which means that an individual's income or savings have no bearing on whether they qualify for the benefit. Although many people may be rejected for PIP despite having a disability or chronic health condition, the assessment process can be difficult.

The method that DLA is evaluated has undergone some adjustments as a result of the implementation of PIP. DLA claims are no longer being accepted; instead, individuals must submit PIP applications. Existing DLA claimants will undergo a PIP reassessment, however the government has announced that this process will take place gradually over several years.

In conclusion, understanding the changes to DLA due to the introduction of PIP is crucial for anyone looking to claim disability benefits. PIP assesses a person's ability to carry out a range of everyday activities and how they manage their daily living and mobility needs. The assessment is based on a points system, and the amount of benefit paid is based on the number of points a person is awarded. The PIP assessment can be a challenging and stressful experience, and many people may be denied the benefit despite having a disability or long-term health condition.

2: DECIDING WHETHER TO CLAIM DLA

For many persons with disabilities, deciding whether to apply for Disability Living Allowance (DLA) can be a challenging decision. DLA can, on the one hand, offer much-needed financial assistance to assist in defraying the costs of care and support. However, applying for DLA can be challenging, and doing so carries some risk.

Before considering a DLA claim, it is essential to understand the prerequisites. To qualify for DLA, an individual must experience difficulties in mobility or engaging in daily activities due to a disability or health condition. Additionally, the condition should be expected to persist for a minimum of one year.

Once a person has established their eligibility, it's critical to weigh the advantages and drawbacks of filing for DLA. DLA can offer financial assistance to pay the costs of care and support, which is one of its main advantages. This can involve things like personal care, house modifications, and mobility aids.

However, obtaining DLA carries certain hazards as well. For instance, despite having a disability or ongoing medical condition, many people are denied the benefit and the evaluation process can be challenging and frustrating. The amount of DLA a person receives can affect their eligibility for other benefits like Housing Benefit and Council Tax Reduction, thus requesting DLA can also have an impact on those benefits.

Before making a choice, people should carefully consider the advantages and disadvantages of requesting DLA. For some persons, the dangers and difficulties of the assessment procedure may be worth the financial assistance provided by DLA. Others might find it more advantageous to rely on different types of support, such social care services or help from family and friends.

It's crucial to comprehend how DLA affects other benefits. A person's eligibility for other benefits, such as Carer's Allowance or Universal Credit, may improve in some circumstances if they apply for DLA. However, in other circumstances, a person's access to other benefits, particularly means-tested payments, may be impacted by the amount of DLA they get.

Overall, choosing to file for DLA is a complex decision that necessitates carefully weighing the risks and rewards involved. It is critical for people to comprehend their benefit eligibility as well as how claiming DLA may affect other benefits. While DLA may be able to offer much-needed financial assistance, it is crucial to balance this against the dangers and difficulties of the evaluation process.

It's critical to weigh the advantages and drawbacks of applying for DLA as well as the potential effects on other facets of an individual's life. A person's eligibility for other forms of financial assistance, such as grants or loans, may be impacted by their DLA claim, for instance. Additionally, because some businesses may regard DLA as a barrier to employment, it may affect a person's capacity to work.

It is crucial to observe that DLA doesn't suggest having a go at inferring that a singular's compensation or venture reserves don't impact their capability to their benefit. This can be an immense advantage for people who have limited money-related resources, as they could be equipped for DLA regardless of whether or not they have a fairly large association compensation.

One critical idea while picking whether to ensure DLA is the impact that the benefit can have on a person's overall flourishing. For certain people with handicaps, the money-related assistance given by DLA with canning has a colossal impact on their own fulfilment. This can consolidate things like having the choice to bear the expense of home changes, adaptability, or individual thought, which can help people live even more independently and without any problems.

Moreover, the most widely recognized approach to ensuring DLA can be a valuable practice in self-assessment. The application connection anticipates that individuals should contemplate their own abilities and cutoff points, which can help with recognizing areas where additional assistance may be required. This can be particularly valuable for people who may be reluctant to search for help or who have hardly any insight into the organizations and resources that are open to them.

Finally, the decision to ensure DLA will depend upon an extent of individual components, including a person's capability and money-related situation, and by and large, individuals should carefully consider their decisions and search for advice and sponsorship based on the circumstances. This could integrate chatting with a benefits guide, a clinical benefits capable, or other insufficient affiliations who can provide guidance and sponsorship all through the application process.

All things considered, picking whether to ensure DLA is a confounded decision that requires careful consideration of the benefits and perils inferred. While DLA can offer really fundamental financial assistance to people with handicaps, it is crucial to understand the impact that ensuring the benefit can have on various pieces of a person's life. By measuring the benefits and risks of ensuring DLA and searching for direction and support contingent upon the circumstances, individuals can reach an informed decision about whether to seek the benefit.

3: PREPARING FOR THE APPLICATION PROCESS

Applying for Disability Living Allowance (DLA) or Personal Independence Payment (PIP) can be a daunting and stressful process for many people with disabilities. However, with careful preparation and support, it is possible to navigate the application process successfully. In this chapter, we will discuss some key steps to help you prepare for the application process and increase your chances of a successful claim.

How to Prepare for the Application Process

Planning for the DLA or PIP application process includes a few key stages, including gathering documentation and proof, understanding the application cycle, and looking for help and encouragement on a case-by-case basis. Critical stages to consider include:

1. Gathering Documentation and Proof: While planning for your DLA or PIP application, it is essential to assemble all the important documentation and proof that you should uphold. This can incorporate clinical records, solutions, care plans, letters from medical

41

services experts, and whatever other important documentation shows your degree of need. Having this documentation coordinated and promptly accessible can make the application cycle smoother and increase your odds of coming out on top.

2. Understanding the Application Interaction: It is essential to look into the application cycle before you start. This can assist you with guessing what's in store and guarantee that you are ready for each phase of the cycle. You can find data about the application cycle on the gov.uk site, which gives a bit-by-bit manual for the application interaction and what's in store.

3. Seeking Help and Exhortation: Applying for DLA or PIP can be a mind-boggling and upsetting cycle, and it is vital to look for help and counsel on a case-by-case basis. This might include talking with an advantage counsellor, medical care proficient, or disability association who can give direction and backing all through the application interaction.

Who Can Help with the Application Process

There are several organizations and individuals who can provide support and guidance throughout the DLA or PIP application process. Some key sources of support include:

1. Benefits Advisors: Benefits advisors are professionals who specialize in providing advice and support to people who are applying for benefits, including DLA or PIP. They can help you to understand the eligibility criteria, gather the necessary documentation and evidence, and prepare your application.

2. Healthcare Professionals: Your healthcare professionals can also provide valuable support and advice throughout the application process. This may include providing documentation or evidence of your condition, writing letters of support, or helping you to prepare for the assessment process.

3. Disability Organizations: There are many disability organizations that provide information and support to people with disabilities who are applying for benefits. These organizations can provide guidance on the application process, connect you with

other resources and services, and provide emotional support and advocacy.

What to Expect When You Start Your Claim

Once you have assembled your documentation and proof and are prepared to start your DLA or PIP application, there are a few vital stages to know about. These include:

1. Completing the Application Structure: The application structure for DLA or PIP can be extended and complex, and it is vital to completely disclose your investment and answer every one of the inquiries. It is additionally essential to give as much detail as could reasonably be expected about your condition and what it means for your everyday existence.

2. The Evaluation Cycle: On the off chance that your application is effective, you will be welcome to go to an appraisal to decide your qualification for the advantage. The evaluation will include an eye-to-eye meeting with a medical care professional who will ask you questions about your condition and what it means for your regular routine.

3. Receiving a Choice: After your evaluation, you will get a choice about your eligibility for DLA or PIP. On the off chance that your case is fruitful, you will be granted the advantage, and the sum you get will be based on your degree of need.

Understanding the Importance of Documentation and Evidence

While applying for DLA, it is vital to give as much proof as could reasonably be expected to help your case. The proof ought to show what your inability means for your everyday life and portability needs. Giving pertinent and precise proof can make the difference between having your case supported or dismissed.

There are various sorts of proof that you can give to help your case. These incorporate clinical proof, care supplier articulations, and explanations from loved ones who can validate what your incapacity means for your regular routine. It is critical to accumulate all the essential proof prior to presenting your case, as this can assist you in staying away from delays in the appraisal cycle.

Clinical proof is one of the main sorts of proof that you can give to help your case. This incorporates reports from your GP, expert specialists, or medical clinic release synopses. Your clinical proof ought to plainly frame the idea of your condition, the side affects you experience, and what it means for your regular routine.

Notwithstanding clinical proof, care provider explanations can likewise be helpful. These assertions can emerge from medical services experts, social specialists, or other consideration suppliers who have been associated with your consideration. Care supplier explanations ought to feature the degree of care and support you expect consistently because of your incapacity.

Articulations from loved ones who know all about your condition and what it means for your day-to-day existence can likewise be useful. These assertions ought to give a legitimate and exact record of what your inability means for your life. Loved ones can give insight into what your condition has meant for your public activity, capacity to work, and everyday exercises.

It is critical to assemble all the fundamental proof and submit it with your case structure. This guarantees that the DWP has all the important data expected to make an exact decision on your case. Submitting fragmented or lacking proof can prompt delays in the evaluation cycle or even a dismissal of your case.

As well as social affair proof, it is vital to keep duplicates of all the proof you submit. This incorporates duplicates of any clinical reports, care supplier articulations, and other supporting records. Keeping duplicates of your proof can be useful on the off chance that you want to provide extra data during the evaluation interaction.

In general, understanding the significance of documentation and proof is basic while getting ready for the DLA application process. Assembling and submitting exact and significant proof can assist with supporting your case and increase the possibilities of an effective result.

4: COMPLETEING THE DLA APPLICATION FORM

Whenever you have chosen to apply for Disability Living Allowance (DLA), the subsequent stage is to finish the application structure. The application structure is a fundamental piece of the interaction, as it is utilized to accumulate data about your condition and what it means for your regular routine. In this section, we will give you a bit-by-bit manual for finishing the application structure, ways to finish it up precisely and completely, what to remember for the structure to help your case, and what to do on the off chance that you really want assistance with the application cycle.

Step-by-Step Guide to Completing the Application Form

The DLA application form is a lengthy document that can be overwhelming. However, it is crucial to take the time to complete it carefully and thoroughly to ensure that your claim is assessed correctly. Here is a step-by-step guide to completing the application form:

1. Read the guidance notes carefully: Before you start filling out the application form, read

the guidance notes that come with it. The guidance notes provide you with important information about how to fill out the form, the eligibility criteria, and the types of evidence you need to provide to support your claim.

2. Fill out the personal details section: The first section of the application form asks for your personal details, such as your name, address, date of birth, and National Insurance number.

3. Provide details about your condition: The next section of the form asks for details about your condition, such as the name of your condition, when you were diagnosed, and how it affects your daily life.

4. Complete the care needs section: The care needs section of the form asks you to provide details about the help you need with your daily living activities, such as getting dressed, washing, and cooking.

5. Complete the mobility needs section: The mobility needs section of the form asks you to provide details about how your condition affects your ability to move around, such as walking or using public transport.

6. Provide supporting evidence: You should include any relevant medical evidence to support your application, such as letters from your GP or consultant, prescription lists, and test results.

7. Sign and date the form: Once you have completed the form, make sure you sign and date it.

Tips for Filling Out the Form Accurately and Thoroughly

It is essential to fill out the DLA application form as accurately and thoroughly as possible. Here are some tips to help you:

1. Be honest: It is essential to be honest when filling out the application form. You should provide accurate information about your condition and how it affects your daily life.

2. Provide specific examples: Providing specific examples of how your condition affects you can help to support your claim. For example, if you have difficulty washing, you could explain that you need help to get in and out of the bath or shower.

3. Be detailed: The more detailed information you provide, the better. You should provide as much information as possible about your condition and how it affects your daily life.

4. Use additional pages: If you need more space to provide information, you can use additional pages. Make sure you label each page with your name and National Insurance number.

What to Include in the Form to Support Your Claim

To help your DLA guarantee, you ought to incorporate any important proof that shows what your condition means for your regular routine. Here are some instances of proof that you might wish to include:

1. Medical proof: You ought to incorporate any clinical proof that upholds your case, like letters from your GP or advisor, remedy records, and experimental outcomes.

2. Care arrangement: On the off chance that you have a consideration plan, you ought to incorporate it with your application.

3. Supporting letters: You might wish to ask companions, relatives, or carers to compose a

letter supporting your case. These letters ought to make sense of how your condition influences your regular routine and the effect it has on your capacity to complete ordinary exercises.

4. Personal proclamation: You ought to incorporate an individual explanation into your application structure. This assertion ought to make sense, as it would be natural for you to know what your condition means for your day-to-day existence and what troubles you face.

5. Financial proof: You ought to incorporate any monetary proof that is applicable to your case, like bank proclamations, lease or home loan articulations, and service bills.

6. Education or business proof: Assuming you are in training or business, you ought to incorporate proof that shows what your condition means for your capacity to go to classes or work.

It is essential to incorporate as much proof as could reasonably be expected to help your case. This will assist the DWP in understanding what your condition means for your regular routine and arriving at a precise conclusion about your qualification for DLA.

While finishing the DLA application structure, it is essential to request your investment and to respond to all inquiries as precisely and completely as could really be expected. The application structure can be extensive and may require a ton of data; however, it is critical to give as much detail as could be expected.

<u>Here are some tips for filling out the form:</u>

1. Read the directions cautiously: Prior to beginning the structure, ensure you read the guidelines cautiously. This will assist you in understanding what data is required and how to respond to each question.

2. Use extra sheets if essential: On the off chance that there isn't sufficient room on the structure to give all the data required, you can append extra sheets.

3. Be genuine. It is vital to be straightforward while finishing the structure. Try not to overstate your condition, yet don't minimize it, all things considered.

4. Focus on what your condition means for your day-to-day existence: While addressing the inquiries, centre around what your condition means for your capacity to do ordinary exercises, like dressing, washing, and getting ready for feasts.

5. Provide models: While portraying what your condition means for your regular routine, give explicit models. For instance, assuming you experience issues strolling, describe how far you can stroll prior to encountering agony or weakness.

In the event that you want assistance finishing the application structure, you can contact the DWP for help. You can likewise ask a companion, relative, or support worker to help you. It is critical to guarantee that the data given on the structure is exact and mirrors the effect of your condition on your day-to-day routine.

5: THE DLA ASSESSMENT PROCESS

The DLA assessment process is a crucial part of the DLA application process. It is during this stage that your application will be reviewed, and a decision will be made about whether or not you are eligible for DLA. In this chapter, we will discuss how the DLA assessment process works, what happens during a DLA assessment, what to expect during a DLA assessment, and how to prepare for a DLA assessment.

How the DLA Assessment Process Works

When you have finished your DLA application structure and submitted it to the DWP, a chief will review your application. On the off chance that your application meets the qualification standards for DLA, you will be welcome to go for an up-close and personal evaluation. The motivation behind this appraisal is to assemble more data about what your handicap means for your day-to-day existence and to decide the degree of help you want.

The DLA appraisal is completed by an autonomous medical services professional who is prepared to survey inability. The medical services proficient will be either a specialist or a medical caretaker and will have experience working with individuals who have disabilities. The medical care proficient will utilize the data you have provided on your DLA application structure, alongside any extra data from your clinical records, to survey your degree of inability.

What Happens During a DLA Assessment

The DLA evaluation is generally completed at an appraisal place. The evaluation might happen in a confidential room or in a social setting. During the evaluation, the medical services expert will ask you questions about your incapacity and what it means for your everyday existence. They may likewise request that you complete a few actual undertakings, like standing or sitting, to survey your portability.

The medical services proficient will utilize the data assembled during the evaluation to finish a report, which will be shipped off to the DWP. This report will remember the medical care professional's perspective on your degree of handicap and what it means for your day-to-day existence.

What to Expect During a DLA Assessment

It is natural to feel nervous or anxious about attending a DLA assessment. However, it is important to remember that the healthcare professional conducting the assessment is there to help you. They want to understand how your disability affects your daily life so they can make an informed decision about your eligibility for DLA.

During the assessment, you will be asked questions about your disability and how it affects your daily life. It is important to answer these questions as honestly and accurately as possible. If you are unsure about a question or need further clarification, do not be afraid to ask for it. The healthcare professional will be happy to explain anything you do not understand.

You may also be asked to carry out some physical tasks during the assessment. These tasks are designed to assess your mobility and the impact your disability has on your ability to carry out daily activities. If you are unable to carry out a task, it is important to let the healthcare professional know. They will take this into account when assessing your level of disability.

<u>How to Prepare for a DLA Assessment</u>

Planning for a DLA evaluation can assist with lessening any uneasiness or anxiety you might feel.

Here are a few hints to assist you with planning for your evaluation:

- Peruse the data given by the DWP about the evaluation interaction. This will assist you in understanding what's in store during the appraisal.

- Take someone with you to the appraisal. Having a companion or relative with you can offer help and reassure you.

- Set up a rundown of the manners by which your incapacity influences your day-to-day routine. This will assist you in answering questions all the more precisely and completely.

- Carry any applicable documentation or proof with you to the evaluation. This might incorporate clinical letters or reports, a consideration plan, or whatever other documentation supports your case for DLA.

- Dress serenely and wear reasonable apparel. Wearing agreeable and appropriate attire for the assessment is significant. Assuming your incapacity influences your versatility, or you experience issues getting dressed, let the assessor know so they can take the proper course of action to help you.

- Show up sooner than expected: Showing up sooner than expected for your appraisal can assist with lessening any tension or stress. It likewise gives you an opportunity to unwind and accumulate your thoughts before your appraisal. Ensure you plan your excursion ahead of time, considering any potential postponements or disturbances to public vehicles.

- Bring a companion or promoter: You reserve the option to bring a companion, relative, or supporter with you to the evaluation. This can offer close-to-home help and assist you in feeling more open during the appraisal. They can likewise take notes and assist with ensuring that all the significant data is covered during the appraisal.

- Tell the truth and be open: During the evaluation, it's vital to tell the truth and be open about what your handicap means for your everyday existence. Try not to minimize your side effects or attempt to misrepresent them, as this can sabotage your validity and limit your possibilities of getting the right degree of help. Be ready to address inquiries concerning your condition, your drug, and any medicines or treatments you get.

- Enjoy reprieves if fundamental: In the event that you really want to have some time off during the appraisal, let the assessor know. They ought to have the option to oblige your requirements and provide appropriate offices if important. Try not to feel compelled to hurry through the evaluation or to respond to questions in the event that you're not feeling well or need a break.

- Trail not too far behind the evaluation: After the appraisal, you ought to get a choice letter illustrating whether you have been granted DLA. In the event that you are discontent with the choice, you reserve the option to challenge it through a reexamination or allure process. Ensure you comprehend your choices and look for guidance from an advantage consultant or backing administration if essential.

All in all, planning for a DLA evaluation can be overwhelming; however, with the right help and readiness, it tends to be a positive and engaging experience. By understanding the appraisal cycle, knowing your freedoms, and telling the truth and being open about your condition, you can expand your possibilities of getting the right degree of help to assist you with dealing with your regular routine.

6: AFTER YOU SUBMIT YOUR APPLICATION

After submitting your DLA application, the next step is to wait for a decision. It can be a stressful time, especially if you rely on the benefit to meet your daily living and mobility needs. In this chapter, we will discuss what you can expect after submitting your application, including the time frame for receiving a decision, how to appeal a decision, and what to include in your appeal. We will also discuss how to ask for a reconsideration of the decision.

Understanding the Time Frame for Receiving a Decision

Subsequent to presenting your DLA application, you will get a choice letter from the Division for Work and Annuities (DWP) expressing your preference regardless of whether you have been granted the advantage. The time span for getting a choice shifts; however, it commonly takes between four and about two months. Now and again, it can take more time, particularly assuming the DWP requires extra data or proof.

It is essential to remember that the DWP's choice isn't conclusive, and you reserve the option to pursue it assuming you can't help contradicting their choice.

How to Appeal a DLA Decision

If you disagree with the decision made by the DWP, you have the right to appeal. The appeal process is a way to challenge the decision and provide additional evidence to support your claim. There are several stages to the appeal process, including mandatory reconsideration and appeal to a tribunal.

Mandatory Reconsideration

Subsequent to presenting your DLA application, you will get a choice letter from the Department for Work and Pensions (DWP) expressing your preference, regardless of whether you have been granted the advantage. The time span for getting a choice shifts; however, it commonly takes between four weeks and about two months. Now and again, it can take more time, particularly assuming the DWP requires extra data or proof.

It is essential to remember that the DWP's choice isn't conclusive, and you reserve the option to pursue it assuming you can't help contradicting their choice.

Appeal to a Tribunal

On the off chance that you are not happy with the compulsory reevaluation choice, you can contact the council. A council is a free body that will survey your case and make a decision in light of the evidence given. To speak to a court, you should complete Form SSCS1 within one month of the date on your required reexamination choice letter.

The council hearing is generally held within 14 weeks of the allure being stopped. You will be advised of the date, time, and area of the meeting. It is essential to go to the meeting, as this is your chance to give extra proof and make sense of your circumstances.

What to Include in Your Appeal

To ensure your appeal is successful, it is important to include as much evidence as possible to support your claim. This evidence could include:

1. Medical evidence: Any medical evidence that supports your claim, such as letters from your GP or consultant, prescription lists, and test results.

2. Care plan: If you have a care plan, you should include it with your appeal.

3. Supporting letters: You may wish to ask friends, family members, or healthcare professionals to provide supporting letters that explain how your condition affects your daily life and mobility.

4. Personal statement: You should provide a personal statement that explains how your condition affects your daily life and mobility. Be specific and provide examples.

5. Any additional evidence: You should include any additional evidence that you believe is relevant to your claim.

It is important to provide all of the evidence you have to support your claim. The tribunal will review all of the evidence before making a decision.

How to Ask for a Reconsideration of the Decision

If you do not want to go through the appeal process, you may also request a reconsideration of the decision. This involves asking the Department for Work and Pensions to look at your case again and consider whether they made the right decision.

To request a reconsideration, you must fill out a form called the SSCS1, which is available on the government's website. You must complete the form within one month of receiving your decision letter.

When completing the form, you should explain why you disagree with the decision and provide any additional evidence that supports your claim. You should also explain why you believe the decision was incorrect and provide any new information that you did not include in your initial application.

Once you have submitted the form, the Department for Work and Pensions will review your case and make a decision. If they change their decision in your favor, you will receive backdated payments for any benefits owed. If the reconsideration process is unsuccessful, you may still appeal the decision to the Tribunal. It is important to note that appealing a decision can be a lengthy process, so it is essential to seek support and advice to help you through the process.

In summary, the process of claiming DLA can be overwhelming and confusing. However, with the right information, preparation and support, you can navigate the system and secure the benefits you are entitled to. Remember to seek advice and support if you are unsure about any part of the process, and do not be afraid to appeal a decision if you believe it is incorrect.

7: RESOURCES AND SUPPORT

Applying for Disability Living Allowance (DLA) can be an overwhelming and overpowering experience, particularly if you are going through it alone. In any case, there are numerous assets and backing administrations accessible to assist you with exploring the DLA application process and then some.

In this section, we will give you data on different assets and backing administrations accessible to you. We will likewise examine how to find neighborhood support administrations and how to get additional assistance with the DLA interaction.

List of Resources and Support Services Available to Disabled People

1. Disability Rights UK: Incapacity Privileges UK is a public cause that assists debilitated individuals and their families with living freely. They offer a large number of administrations, including benefit guidance and backing, instruction and preparation, work administrations, and companion support.

2. Citizens Advice: Residents Guidance gives free, classified, and unbiased counsel on many issues, including benefits, obligations, lodging, and legitimate issues. They have workplaces across the UK and offer support on the web and by phone as well.

3. Scope: Degree is a public foundation that attempts to make this country a superior spot for impaired individuals and their families. They offer a scope of administrations, including benefit exhortation and backing, business administrations, and online local area discussions.

4. Disability Action: Disability Action is a Northern Ireland-based cause that attempts to advance the privileges of crippled individuals and their families. They offer a scope of administrations, including benefits exhortation and backing, work administrations, and preparation and instruction.

5. Disabled Living Foundation (DLF): The DLF gives unprejudiced counsel, data, and preparation on hardware that can assist with everyday living. They offer web-based counselling, data administration, and a helpline for guidance on items.

6. Motability: Motability is a foundation that assists incapacitated individuals with renting a vehicle, bike, or fueled wheelchair through the Motability Plan. The plan offers a scope of vehicles and variations to suit various requirements.

Finding Local Support Services

Numerous neighborhood support administrations are accessible to debilitated individuals and their families. Neighborhood specialists are answerable for offering types of assistance like home variations, social consideration, and gear to assist with everyday residing. You can figure out what administrations are accessible in your space by reaching your nearby chamber or social administrations division.

Notwithstanding neighborhood specialists, there are numerous foundations and non-benefit associations that proposition administrations to incapacitated individuals and their families. You can find neighborhood support administrations via looking on the web or by reaching public causes that deal administrations in your space.

Accessing Further Help with the DLA Process

If you need further help with the DLA process, there are several options available to you. You can contact the DLA helpline for advice and support, or you can seek advice from a benefits adviser or disability support organization.

Benefits advisers can provide free and impartial advice on benefits, including DLA. They can help you to understand the eligibility criteria, guide you through the application process, and provide support if your application is refused.

Disability support organizations can also provide advice and support on benefits and other issues that affect disabled people and their families. They can provide peer support, help with accessing services, and provide information on local support groups and activities.

In conclusion, applying for DLA can be a challenging and confusing process, but there are many resources and support services available to help you through it. Whether you need advice on benefits, help with daily living, or just someone to talk to, there is support available to help you live your life to the fullest. Don't be afraid to reach out for help if you need it – there are people and organizations out there that want to help you.

<u>CONCLUSION</u>

Throughout this book, we have covered a range of topics related to Disability Living Allowance (DLA) and the application process. We hope that this information has been helpful to you in understanding DLA and how to go about claiming it if you are eligible.

To recap, we began by discussing the basics of DLA, including how it works, the eligibility criteria, and the different components of the benefit. We then delved into the differences between DLA and Personal Independence Payment (PIP), as well as the changes that have been made to the benefit system over the years.

Next, we explored the decision to claim DLA, including the benefits and risks of doing so, as well as the impact that claiming DLA may have on other benefits. We then discussed how to prepare for the application process, including gathering evidence and seeking help if needed.

In Chapter 4, we provided a step-by-step guide to completing the DLA application form, with tips for filling it out accurately and thoroughly. Chapter 6 covered what to do after you submit your application, including understanding the time frame for receiving a decision, how to appeal a decision, and how to ask for a reconsideration.

In Chapter 5, we discussed the DLA assessment process, including what to expect during the assessment and how to prepare for it. Finally, in Chapter 7, we provided a list of resources and support services available to disabled people, as well as information on how to find local support and access further help with the DLA process.

Our final advice for readers is to remember that applying for DLA can be a challenging and overwhelming process, but it is important to stay focused and persistent. Remember to seek help and support from friends, family members, and advocacy organizations if needed, and to take the time to gather all of the necessary evidence before submitting your application.

We also encourage anyone who believes they may be eligible for DLA to consider applying. The benefit is there to provide financial support to those who need it and can make a significant difference in the lives of disabled people and their families.

In conclusion, we hope that this book has provided you with the information and guidance you need to understand the DLA application process and make an informed decision about whether to apply.

Remember, if you have any questions or concerns, there are many resources and support services available to help you along the way. Good luck!

<u>ABOUT THE AUTHOR</u>

Teeghan Rhodes is an advocate, author, and dedicated father who embarked on a transformative journey of growth and empowerment when his two children were diagnosed with ADHD and autism. Through his personal experiences, he gained a profound understanding of the importance of advocating for his children, raising awareness, and educating others about special educational needs.

With a candid and empathetic voice, Teeghan motivates and inspires other families to persevere in their advocacy efforts and continue fighting for the best outcomes for their children. He recognizes the challenges that families face and offers guidance, support, and encouragement along their own journeys.

Beyond his writing endeavors, Teeghan finds immense joy in spending quality time with his loved ones. He actively volunteers with organizations that provide support to children with special needs, firmly believing in the power of community and collaboration to make a positive impact. His commitment to raising awareness and providing hope for families facing similar circumstances is unwavering.

Teeghan Rhodes is dedicated to using his voice and experiences to shed light on the EHCP process and empower parents and caregivers to navigate it successfully. His passion for making a difference in the lives of children with special educational needs shines through in his work and his commitment to fostering understanding, compassion, and inclusivity.

TEEGHAN RHODES

Printed in Great Britain
by Amazon

41116837R00046